HANNIBAL

HANNIBAL

poems by

SHAUNA HANNIBAL

Erin,
so nice
to meet
you at !
White Prom.

Shara
AWP Tampa
3/9/18

FORKLIFT_BOOKS

FORKLIFT BOOKS EDITION, NOVEMBER 2017

ISBN 978-0-9995931-5-8

Edited by Matt Hart
Book and cover design by Eric Appleby
Cover illustration by Annelie Carlström
Author photo by Tyrone McCloskey

Cincinnati, Ohio

WWW.FORKLIFTBOOKS.COM

contents

✳

✳

HANNIBAL

I'M SO HOT

I'M SO HOT
BUT I'LL BE WAY HOTTER

Standing over there worried
About everybody's emotions

Immaculate panties
Lacy with expectation

My head full of owls

I'M SO HOT
BUT I'LL BE WAY HOTTER
WHEN I'M 47 IS WHAT I'D TELL MY YOUNGER SELF

When I find myself in an awkward position
usually it involves bad timing
though on the day
the moon broke I was there.

Every once in a while it's as easy
as waking up on fire,

my hope is an insurgent rectangle ignited
luminous particle, small spark.

Go out for tacos. Jump over the air is
brimming with pleasure and land
in the blasphemy courtyard, troubled,
talk about purgatory of stars!
Truly dork supreme
perfectly close to
another way to say
I cannot feel.

I'M SO HOT
BUT I'LL BE WAY HOTTER
WHEN I'M 47 IS WHAT I'D TELL MY YOUNGER SELF
TO SAY TO HERSELF IN THE MIRROR

She walked in on it she could tell
right away what she'd done she was
wearing her heart on her *something*
open wine goody touch her where it all fits
together according to her majesty
with which water falls she's finished
righteously streaming hither

Come wet turn screw whomever
I was wearing my heart on my sleeve when
I walked in on it there was no
question of joining him then as if
orchids dangled off trees or peonies
burned like crumpled tissue set on
fire I turned my back my goodness
asphalt and let the sirens scream

**I'M SO HOT
BUT I'LL BE WAY HOTTER
WHEN I'M 47 IS WHAT I'D TELL MY YOUNGER SELF
TO SAY TO HERSELF IN THE MIRROR
EVERYONE HAS A DREAM**

The light from the setting sun shines
through the cracks in the glass
of forever.

I think this must be what it's like inside
a helium balloon on a clear blue
day in the park.

Someone just made a goddamn big mistake.
Wrong testicle.
But it's February, too early
for the *Chiranthodendron pentadactylon*
to bloom.

**I'M SO HOT
BUT I'LL BE WAY HOTTER
WHEN I'M 47 IS WHAT I'D TELL MY YOUNGER SELF
TO SAY TO HERSELF IN THE MIRROR
EVERYONE HAS A DREAM
OR SOME IDEA OF WHAT SHE WANTS TO BECOME**

Look up from now and see how
the sun, trembling, rises
while I am barely breathing,
lungs unlike anything
that holds oblivion.
It's pretty desolate here,

rising unhurried dim
the new moon shows up the sky barely
manages the usual increments
inimitably appears

to horizon slip and gone
to lie with another night illicit
for being far from where we are
on opposite sides of a divided year.

I'M SO HOT
BUT I'LL BE WAY HOTTER
WHEN I'M 47 IS WHAT I'D TELL MY YOUNGER SELF
TO SAY TO HERSELF IN THE MIRROR
EVERYONE HAS A DREAM
OR SOME IDEA OF WHAT SHE WANTS TO BECOME
I MAKE A LOT OF MISTAKES

Heart edge of the bed what's wrong suddenly

Foolish woman
foolish
woman grasping for the wrong tongue

In the dumb smash I'm not getting anywhere
fast I haven't been with
anyone I know
or don't woo
hoo

Reliable penis

comes lately
disguised as the many-petaled hour

I'M SO HOT
BUT I'LL BE WAY HOTTER
WHEN I'M 47 IS WHAT I'D TELL MY YOUNGER SELF
TO SAY TO HERSELF IN THE MIRROR
EVERYONE HAS A DREAM
OR SOME IDEA OF WHAT SHE WANTS TO BECOME
I MAKE A LOT OF MISTAKES
I MAKE A LOT OF MISTAKES

The motions of the body

tonight at their most

corrupt and tremulous

while all around

the world lovers fight

pretend to believe

when literally all we've got

to do is

I'M SO HOT
BUT I'LL BE WAY HOTTER
WHEN I'M 47 IS WHAT I'D TELL MY YOUNGER SELF
TO SAY TO HERSELF IN THE MIRROR
EVERYONE HAS A DREAM
OR SOME IDEA OF WHAT SHE WANTS TO BECOME
I MAKE A LOT OF MISTAKES
I MAKE A LOT OF MISTAKES
I DON'T CONFUSE MY MANTRAS WITH MY SONGS

French this

Go ahead God

Is dead in the details

Just go right up and

Wink gush

Altogether nonplussed with

Fingers crossed

Behind my back

For there are promises promises

I know I'll never keep

PASSAGE

One of the most depressing things to happen at a modern art museum is to have to decide if you'll enter the small room off to the side you know will be playing a video on an endless loop, because while you don't want to admit it, you really want to watch something on a screen after seeing all that abstraction on the walls. Problem is nine times out of ten the thing in the room lets you down. It has even less of a satisfying story to it than the art and it makes you mad. You get to sit down and veg for a few minutes at least.

This time as I go in, the corridor seems longer and darker than usual. I can't see anything at all for a few seconds and before my eyes can fully adapt I'm facing the blazing screen, instantly transported to the desert of Morocco where a group of women covered head to toe in black despite the brutal sun huddle together digging in the sand with their bare hands to the sound of frantic music by the famous experimental minimalist. I have a sinking feeling almost like *déjà vu*; not being able to see what the women are bent over as they dig reminds me of the scene with the lions in the Ray Bradbury story *The Veldt* I read when I was a kid. The lions are huddled over something in the middle distance of the African grasslands, but you don't know what it is.

In the Bradbury story, ten-year old brother and sister twins, Peter and Wendy, keep going into the veldt via their "nursery" (which is in fact a virtual reality room), preferring the veldt to anywhere else in their futuristic "HappyLife Home." After a while, their parents become concerned the children don't seem to be changing the virtual reality channel to anything else, so they announce they're shutting down the nursery, thereby cutting off the children's access to Africa.

The twins manage to lure their parents into the nursery one last time, and lock them in, whereupon the parents become aware the lions are *eating* something, and the screams they've been hearing lately coming from the African veldt whenever they pass by the nursery are indeed familiar to them, because it's their own voices they're hearing, they're the ones screaming. It's too late though, the parents realize they're locked into a virtual reality becoming terribly real, simultaneously watching themselves being eaten by lions while being eaten by lions on the veldt. You see, it was they the lions were crouched over that whole time.

This is a disturbing thing to think of while sitting in the dark at SFMOMA watching the women in Morocco, who it turns out are urgently digging a grave. We know it's a grave because the video keeps cutting to a line of men processing through the sand toward the women, a swaddled corpse raised above their heads. All the while, the repetitive dissonance of the music is taking its toll and the almost *déjà vu* feeling is making me dizzy. Or maybe it's too much exposure to postmodernism.

I have to get out so I stand up and go to brush sand off my dress. I'm not the original owner of this dress, I don't know if she's still the same size or if she donated it to Goodwill because now she's too big or too small but all infinities are the same size: the infinity of who she was and the infinity of who I am and the infinity of maybe she's dead. Carefully I exit through the dark out to where things are weird enough as it is without Philip Glass being the composer of the score.

DEVOTION

When I take
a mental snapshot
of the sky
I see the colors
of the cosmos,
all of them,
especially
the ones
you don't see
and I store
them away
for later
like so many
darling
grudges.

I navigate
solely

by the light of
the Milky Way,
it's all I need,
so go ahead and
tell me the thing
I didn't know
about
our relationship,
the truth will
set us free
as the little
brown birds
I rescued gently
taking my time
with a T-shirt-covered
broom from
where they'd
gotten themselves
trapped
on the balcony.

NUDE BACCHANTS RIDING PANTHERS

It's all brawn and exultant armpits
for *Nude bacchants riding panthers*,
bronze, height 91.2 cm and 90.2 cm,
respectively, c.1506-1508.
Right arms raised high,
the left dropped alongside
their felines exactly like rodeo riders
on bucking broncos except
the panthers aren't bucking,
they're not doing much of anything
besides catching my eye.

Ripped naked dudes
acting out their double drama
astride big bored cats,
I get it, Michelangelo,
why not go for fantastically weird
when heralding the invention of mannerism?
You may have died wondering
how long you could keep them to yourself.
The answer is the earth's on fire.

COMEBACK

When I hear the scientist explain the difference
between Pleistocene
and conventional rewilding
I know I'll be okay,
that I'm on the planet now
with this person earnest
about his area of expertise.

I love the planet we're on
where we bring back
wolves and back-breed mammoths.

When I see the sheer volume
of velour at the thrift store,
racks and racks of luxurious tracksuits, same thing,
I feel comforted.

Some things feel extra good
when you rub up against them,
especially the ones you don't expect
to have a renaissance
in your personal life.

That ex, you assumed you'd never
feel his skin again.
Sweet burn of artificial turf.
When I say I don't want to I
change my mind I
get down on my knees.

MACHU PICCHU

The broken-off boob
on the 11th century
statue makes me grateful
to be unbreakable
and clothed, not missing
any body parts to speak of
just a lot of eggs that
matured and made it out
of my ovaries without
becoming anything
more complicated than that
and a few that did hook up
and get a lot further,
and I wanted there to be new life
growing inside me,
and I didn't.

Today I won't die
posing for a selfie
at Machu Picchu
or try to become something I'm not,
like for example a mother.
My breasts are soft,
still perky, feel good to the touch
and you're supposed to touch them,
unlike those of the Hindu goddess,
or I should say the one of hers
that's intact, she, kept behind glass
at the museum, he, with his iPhone out
in front of him, ecstatic
to arrive at the top
of the Incan citadel
and a lot of good that did him.

CHIMERA

The lemur lifts his chin and pops his collar
in anticipation of the leap then
appears to demur and
I'm totally not surprised
even as I can't believe my eyes.
True enough, jumping prowess
is no advantage stuck out
in the open like this, no trees in sight.
We are far from Madagascar.

A small animal with
pointy fox-like muzzle
sitting on its haunches
in the middle of an intersection
is gonna get hit by a car
sure as I'm standing here
blinking against the sun,
clearly faint with hunger,
not seeing straight.

Errands done, on the way home
I pass the open door of the 99 cent store,
breathe in that blast of

ingeniously mass-produced plastic,
stop. Turn around and walk by
again, slow, really fill
my lungs with what it means
to be human.

PSH

He had a rare ability to illuminate the varieties of
human ugliness. No one ever did it so beautifully.

—*A.O. Scott*

When Philip Seymour Hoffman says "death"
in the movie I'm bored with
up til then, I imagine a supercut
hitting the Internet
of him saying "death"
every time he did.
I try to let myself feel
what it's like now that he's gone
for those of us who loved him
but didn't know him
and before long up floats an idea
for a pointless GIF
distracting me from any discomfort
that may have begun to set in.
I wish I could poke my brain
with a stick; instead I try again
to see him with
no needle in his arm, brilliant, okay
insofar as any of us are,

and really all I wanted was for
Robin Williams to be satisfied.

KING OF HEARTS

The *King of Hearts* playing card
separated from its deck I spot
on my walk to work early this morning
    isn't merely spooky

            it feels occult

When you're waiting for a new heart, Dean Young
wrote, you're waiting for someone to die
and I think of that when I see the card,

how it reminds me in a way of the death
we're all waiting for   my death, your death
everybody's death I guess

how I don't get what that one card
and only that one card
is doing in the middle of the intersection,
    where the rest of the deck went

The *King of Hearts* is the one
holding a sword behind his head is
not dead yet

Love is
   the greatest power in the universe and
no one knows this better than the King

I am the Angel
of my worser nature
I know   and don't
know why I always have to
feel like I'm hurtling toward the abyss

This is not a soft story and it hasn't been
for a while
         Try to smile
invitingly
when I'm depressed,
hold the sword a little farther
to the left

TOC

I can't tell if it's waves crashing or music
for a post-apocalyptic happy hour.

When a French horn signals diminishing returns,
is it sexier to look inconsolable or angry in response?

It's getting late.
I would make a grander statement but I'm afraid.

I used to be a dragged out, but not yet opened, trunk
until you opened me up and now

I'm the table of contents of
A Vindication of the Rights of Woman—

the prevailing opinion of a sexual character discussed.
The same subject continued.

The difference between lusting after
and lusting before you
might mean life or death.

It feels like there should not be bleeding
from the top of the head.

Not pudding after but *instead of* dinner.
I turn my back and how easily you disappear.

A woman dies in a fire after lighting candles
for her imaginary boyfriend,

which is very sad. Mine
are always all too real and

the fire never bright enough
to make anything more clear.

To try to understand the difference between us
I stay up too late.

To get rid of the dark circles under my eyes
I paint my heart white.

SOFT ROBOT

You see yourself as a brunette
is what she said.
I could object
but don't because
I always get hung up
wondering why they're saying
the surprising things they say,
other people, and forget to.

Scientists are building a cyborg stingray,
synthetic animal, whose real rat heart cells contract
one after the other
when exposed to light
and I don't know how to feel about it.

Technically it's a soft robot,
a small step toward synthetic cognition.
All I've ever wanted to build
is a less—or *more*—oblivious boyfriend.

I get goosebumps on my thighs now,
didn't used to get goosebumps on my thighs,

and this is brand-new:
I spray synthetic estrogen on the insides of my wrists.

I'm building castles in the air
but also keep
accumulating turn-ons
and that's not too bad I guess.
If any more of the cat body
disappears behind the drapes
I'll have to go after her I swear.

ROUND UP

I'm about to go and stare at a billboard for free-range chicken for an hour and call it a poem, the raw chicken a weird post-production pink is fascinating and freaks me out. When I get home I'll finish reading the thing I saved about the woman planning to film her own abortion. Wow! It'll strike me that I could say something about abortion in a poem, could say something about not wanting to film myself having one for starters. I can almost hear the roto-rooter sound the machine makes, it'd be a sick kind of PSA or spoof horror flick, cold open on the side of the exam table, all you hear is the chugging. "Round Up" comes to mind, the amusement ride consisting of a circular horizontal platform with a vertical cage-like wall around the edge. The ride starts out by spinning until the centrifugal force is enough to push people against the wall. Then the people go from spinning horizontally to spinning almost vertically anyhow I haven't been on one of those rides in a long time but remembering the feeling of being slammed against the sides reminds me of abortion except it's in reverse, instead of being pushed you're getting pulled out but not all of you, just the heartbreaking part.

JERK

Let
       me
carry
       you
in
       my
paper
       boat
propelled
       by
paper
       oars
the
       swift
way
       up
the
       alembic
of
       my
mind

HOMO

I can describe what I can't see
is one way I know,
mad genus [sic] late *sapien*
telling you what's good:
how my ass looks
to the guy behind me
as I wait for the light
before crossing the street
on my way to therapy,
totally fine object of
late afternoon reverie
half-squinting as we
pitch ourselves up Market.

ENDLESS SUMMER

The man who harassed you before harasses you again
which affects you more than you think it should
and you hate that. You've waited too long
for a haircut and can't get an appointment.
The place you usually go is closed,
you're here instead, in a blue booth, it's early still
there's hardly a din,
you have a little alcohol. A lovely friend
pops into your head just
as you notice you're not getting anywhere
at the table with your moleskine
open to the words "and no dancing."
But hold on—that you're even here with
your notebook open could be
construed as a sign of mental health.
Plus your pen is pointing due north,
promise of even greater feng shui.
You picked out some really good stone
fruit and berries today!
That man who harassed you? He won't
see the next century either.
Somewhere past these *aha* moments
is a boundless fugue

no small amount of mini
chocolate chips spilt out onto the pages can fix
but you've got your mess down,
got it down to this tiny space,
to where it fits
on the head of a pin now
keep still and no dancing.

ATTACHMENT

Today in the back of the bus there were some teenagers holding dear little kittens and one who was eating mac 'n' cheese with his fingers out of the glass of a French press. The kittens were mewling and the teenagers were clutching them close to their chests.

An old woman said in a fake French accent "When zey are small zey are zo irresistible, adorable, zo desirable, zes, zen zey grow up and zere are raccoons and zen zey eat zem."

One of the kids said "I can't wait for football season to start." Another, who wasn't holding a kitten, said "If I had one I'd torture it, I'd give it to my dog and [laughs]." Someone handed her the orange stripey boy kitten and she petted him softly and cooed into his tiny translucent ear.

The teenager had him in the crook of her right arm. She put her left hand up to him, palm out, started tapping his right paw, then his left, saying, "Paddy Cake Paddy Cake Baker's Man Bake Me A Cake As Fast As You Can," forgetting such gestures mean nothing to the kitten who has no hands himself, and no song, until she looked up and saw people were staring. She blushed then snarled. She took the kitten firmly by the scruff of his tiny neck and held him out the open window the way a mother cat does.

A HORSE WITH NO NAME

Too much attention enrages a swan.

—Amelia Gray

Not enough color in your pee, salt in your tears,
barely register a pulse, eidolon you can only go

in two directions:
monochrome or invisible,

one hue or none, the choice is
show up or disappear.

When you pretend you're being watched is it
paranoid or companionable?

Always being able to see someone
out of the corner of your eye

or imagine they're nearby,
possibly glancing at you,

that's what it's like having a cat.
Or writing in a café, but you're not in a café

and your cat died three years ago.
Instead you buy an *Angel de la Guardia* novena candle,

keep it where it flickers away
in your peripheral vision

never letting your eyes rest, it makes you feel
less alone at night, all those thoughts

of indeterminate origin,
small unsolved mysteries adding up.

When you look at the stars,
you're mostly looking at the past

because a lot of the stars you see
are already dead. When you tell someone

you went through a dark period
in your life and they ask when was that

you say two hours ago.
Time, is on your side.

MOOD

I hang my pretty panties
from the small plastic fan
clamped to the shelf
and whirring softly
above your bed,
gusset against grill,
to dry out quicker
so I can put them back on
and get out of here
because all I want to do now

is go home and toast
an everything bagel
and eat it with lots of butter,
propped up against three pillows
with a book
in my own bed
and so what if I find
poppy seeds
between the sheets
tomorrow.

POCKET ROCKET

My friend had an unusual problem she needed to
solve before her flight:
how to bring a sex toy with her
when she returns to that authoritarian socialist state
where she's been living.
My problem's not as exotic, it's

How do I get you to
keep
fucking
me
but
stop
liking me so much/never kiss me again?
I'm sitting here at the bar seeing if I can
figure it out before you show up for a drink.

I don't know if my friend's trick worked.
What she did was she went to Good Vibes,
asked for a vibrator that doesn't look like a vibrator
and was sold a hard
slick pretty purple object
with squared-off sides.

Trying to imagine what the customs agent
might be fooled into thinking it was
as I held it in my hand the day before she left,
I couldn't help
wishing it had a carabiner attached
like maybe it could pass as something outdoorsy
that gets you out of a jam.
I think she ended up taking
the battery out temporarily,
filling the barrel with breath mints.

How absurd you can't re-enter some places
with a personal massager in your pocket.

Sometimes I wish I'd never returned to
the foreign country that is your brain.
I wonder if we'll have sex or if today
will be the day I decide
I'm not doing it.

DIRTY WORD

The Reverse French Manicure
has the same proportion of nude
to white as the French Manicure
only the white semi-circle
is at the base of the nail
instead of the tip.
At the base where
on your natural nail
those crescent moons
lunula rise up.
The Reverse French
in effect gives you
upside-down lunula.
It's a sneaky trick.

Uvula's another word
that sounds dirty
for a part of the body
that typically is not.
What you can reach with
your uvula's not much,
it's too far back
at the soft palate

of your mouth.
A lot of things don't get
to ever come into contact
with each other.
Too bad your bony *cochlea*
will never know the feeling
deep inside my gut.

PRIVATE LIFE

No one's looking, so which you eats too much
of the fancy cheese and which one ignores the cat?
The tree in the yard next door is
sprouting new leaves that come out looking tough,
demanding attention from February.
You'd think the unseasonably hot sun
might mitigate your *crushing ennui*
but ennui doesn't crush,
more like the *crushing repressed rage* you feel lately but no
you're glad to see it's supposed to rain Wednesday.

Gibbous moon faint in the midday sky
forms enough of a circle to get its drift across
though not the same wispy drift of clouds
whose part of the sky nearly touches the part of the sky
where the moon's semi-circle leaves off.

How good/bad you are at fathoming
the size of the universe
is a question worth asking
the version of yourself who paints her nails black,
black she tells herself
to match her black black heart,

how emo, better yet black
as all the black holes that ever existed combined!
You can wrap your head around that amount of space
or the lachrymose
and now the careful calculations
have foretold how stars perish
you feel like you can make it out of this alive.

Just a whiff of acrimony
magic
lust
burnt feeling
on
the
tongue
like you get from eating too much pineapple.
Bet you could smell the ozone lets you know
a storm's on the way if you stay
out here on the master patio long enough.
At least you'll see it coming from a long way off.

WING LEE

Tiny man
reeking of cigarettes
who just sat down beside me,
I want to tell you something:
My outrageously white
and fluffy
steamed BBQ pork bun
(Char Siu Bao)
extant moments ago
is an ode
to your sad little lungs.
I promise I did
them justice.

HUMP DAY

The way I hold you in my mind is like catching fog
when it's coming down so fast
it looks like it's falling
meaning I'm trying to but you slip right through.

I don't know what to do. The tiny bummers and
could-almost-be bummers
of my day get mixed up with the more significant feels.
I just want to be alone so I can get dim sum to go
and eat it on my way home out of those little
non-food grade plastic bags they put it in.

I put my nose too close to a perfume insert
in the October issue of *Glamour*
and I can't get the smell out even though
I washed my face twice.

The packaging on the dark chocolate with
sea salt & almond nougat
candy bar should not be covered in green swirls
because that makes it seem like mint.
Good thing I noticed in the store because what if

by accident I'd bought the other one
with almond-colored swirls which was actually mint?
Ick.

The young excitable man in the dream kept trying
to convince me what a big ass I have
until I believed him.

When are you gonna believe me I know how sexy I am?
C'mon now, you have to stop touching me
so I can go back to sleep.

I REMEMBER

Calamari Fritter is takeout item #9.
I left my husband, not the other way around.
David Bowie died.
Did I leave my husband? On second thought

soaking red onion in Tapatío was a weird idea,
but it wasn't mine.
Tom Waits is alive.
Tom Waits is alive.

Yes, I'm sure I did.

HANNIBAL

I will either find a way, or make one.

—*Hannibal Barca (247-182 BCE),*
Carthaginian general who crossed the Alps
on elephants in an attempt to defeat Rome

I don't know about you but I'm scared

I'm going about it all wrong.

It's possible I have a tragically

bad attitude. I say *asshole* under my breath

followed a little louder by *fucking asshole*

then get mad at myself and

the whole world.

Open up my veins to reveal

how many pairs of leggings I should own

and let me know so I can quit while I'm ahead,

though maybe it's too late—I already bought

the ones that went crazy-viral overnight

and when they arrived three months later

having been constructed

out of recycled water bottles

at the eco-friendly factory

with humane working conditions

in Taiwan I didn't try them on.

Shipped all that way and I'm staving off

the moment when I'm most at risk

of feeling ridiculous

imagining my butt will look just too big.

Haven't got up quite the right bite-me attitude

for wearing leggings outside the house;

in this way I refuse to participate fully in society.

Still I'm going around

looking at other women

and having bad thoughts about my body,

counting the ways it's not like theirs

and my hair, it always

looks sort of terrible

no matter what I do whatever I feel like

I want to puke that's how I can tell I'm alive.

Everything looks unfamiliar the rest of the day.

Bad posture the leitmotif, unanticipated consequence

thereof: slouch wrinkles on my chest. I mean, really?

If I'd known that'd be a sign of aging maybe I would've

stood up straight.

I can't always tell what's going on with my lips

when I've got lipgloss on,

putting shine to my Resting Bitch Face

which in my case

comes off more like resting sad face but

I don't get to be either angry or sad

according to the man in the street

who tells me to smile.

*

I can't

dance.

Yet I'm always getting put on

the invite to BURN DOWN the DiSCO!

dance parties my fling from 17 years ago

DJs.

This morning I was interested in finding out

what the common problem is

according to the pajama brand

and not the Supreme Court decision

on abortion access in Texas.

I needed to know if I have the common problem

so I could decide what to do about it

in the privacy of my home.

Maybe the problem is I know I'll be okay

no matter who I'm with, maybe I should be more

committed, stick it out, not worry

about what happens before things start to get ugly

or after.

I like a pithy dessert menu.

All these parts of myself are sore.

Because the Russian ahead of me orders the sweet

cheese pastry I order the sweet cheese pastry.

Shame is holding the hurt tight against my body

with the itty-bitty arms of a hamster

or T. rex meaning

I can't.

✳

Surprised the next day when details come back

like how some of his luscious black hair got caught

in my mouth as he swung away

from snuffling my neck

the young hot guy at the party

who looks adorably like Frank Zappa.

How did it happen I was alone in the coatroom

with him?

I remember he asked a good question:

Why are you laughing?

His, the most difficult kiss to steal, he wouldn't

give me his lips,

but why am I even trying to be kissed by this person

how absurd is this

is what I was thinking and what cracked me up.

Sometimes I look in the mirror and I don't see myself

and I wonder if that happens to other people,

probably not the ones you can tell practice

looking at themselves in the mirror.

When I see it's not the me I want to see

I make my eyes soft make my mouth softer.

It hurts to smile

so I smile bigger.

✳

Try not to take his eternal optimism personally.

Put on my stratosphere suit for going down

the miniature deer rabbit hole on Etsy or listen to

sad songs from one of my exes' bands on repeat.

Write about mixed feelings.

I think he likes me. Or he likes his idea of me,

which is maybe better,

or I could pose that as a shrugged-shoulder-helium-

voiced question, Which is maybe better?

You know when you think you feel something

because you're expecting to feel it

versus feeling the actual thing

you're feeling which you didn't expect?

I can still feel your breath when I turn my back.

I eat the chocolate like it'll save me

because it does;

past failures to produce low-fat chocolate

are deeply related

to the basic science of soft matter.

This is not a soft story and it hasn't been for a while.

My anxiety about choosing the right teary-eyed emoji

is caught up in what was supposed to happen

versus what actually happened.

I can still feel your hand on my waist.

*

I'm looking for a fake leather jacket to replace my
fake leather jacket.

I say hooray not hurray.

Self-loathing with beauty.

She does it with such beauty.

Still life with self-loathing.

Let's do this en plein air so I don't get scared.

I can still feel your arm on my shoulder.

The cold doesn't bother me anyway.

How do I look?

Keep having sex.

*

Scientists have been studying the exhaled

breath of movie audiences

because we broadcast how we feel out into the air

in the form of chemical signals.

What happens in front of the green screen

besides everything?

On the beach an hour after sunset, no one else

around, we make trite observations about the size

of the waves. We're being good-natured with each

other, both really relaxed in the new dark, it feels

nice to be nice and nice with eyes closed to walk a

little too close to the edge of the tide not knowing

if it's going out or coming in. No wind in the grass,

warm sheltered dunes.

I forget to breathe, to feel my heart beat.

thanks,

Thank you to the editors of the publications where some of these words have appeared: *Big Bell*; *Forklift, Ohio*; *jubilat*; *McSweeney's Internet Tendency*; and *Verse Daily*.

Thank you, Matt Hart. Whenever I got lost you found me. I'm forever grateful.

Thank you, Dean Young.

Thank you, Laura Kasischke.

Thank you, Eric Appleby.

Thank you, Tricia Suit.

Thank you, Marian Joycechild.

Thank you, Annelie Carlström.

Thank you teachers, editors, mentors, exes, and friends—each in your own way, at one time or another—for your generosity, support and kindness. I know it wasn't always easy... Alex Austin, Charles Baxter, Anselm Berrigan, Richenda Brim, Davy Carren, David Clark, Tom Clark, Russell Dillon, Scott Donahue, Garrick Duckler, Roger Fanning, Cal Fischler, Geraldine Foote, Jeff Gauthier, Tracy Goodnight, Amy Grimm, Ray Halliday, Matthea Harvey, Lyn Hejinian, Kevin Killian, Michele Kirk, Li-Young Lee, Gary Lilley, Jill Marquis, Laura Matthews, Tyrone McCloskey, Gary Miranda, Naomi Shihab Nye, Kevin Opstedal, Peg Alford Pursell, Anupama Rao, Cesar Rubio, David Rutschman, Christian Schmit, Ed Skoog, Tom Sleigh, Kim Stafford, Ellen Stauder, Wendy Stein, Jeff Swartz, Robert Thomas, Christine Thornhill, Kenneth Traynor, Peter Turchi, Rachel Uris, Kimberly Voelker, Ellen Bryant Voight, Alice Vosmek, Sladjana Vuckovic, Canon Wing.

My mom & dad, Mary Anne and George Hannibal.

My heart, Xandréa Reynolds and my heart, Xyah Kismet Casey.

This book is for my sister, Anna. I love you more than anything ever and always.

Shauna Hannibal lives in San Francisco.
This is her first book.

Made in the USA
San Bernardino, CA
26 January 2018